To every child that loves and want to learn
more about plants, fruits, and vegetables.

Faith In Your GARDEN

Written By: Faith Godfrey

Hi, my name is Faith, and I will teach you everything you should know about plants today!

**Plants are good for you and me.
Plants all grow by watering seeds!**

If you want to make sure your plants grow right, they must get plenty sunlight.

Plants grow things we can smell with our noses, like Dandelions, and Roses!

Plants are deliciously good.
Plants are used to make a variety of foods!

Variety means a lot!

Plants make awesome décor, just thought I should mention. Now, let's make our way to the kitchen!

Décor is just some fancy word adults use for decorations.

**Apples gives us apple pie,
lemons make lemonade, Oh my!**

Carrots, onions, and tomatoes are yummy! They're good for your eyes, heart and tummy!

Could you imagine growing a garden like the one above? Filled with all the things you love!

Are you excited about growing a garden? Here's a few tips to get things started:

1. You can start your garden *inside* your home, using vegetables, or fruit as a compost.
2. Once you see your plants sprouting, it's time for them to go to the *outside* garden.
3. Outside, you'll begin to see, your veggies and fruits bloom beautifully.

Gardening is fun either with parents or friends. Don't wait, let your gardening begin!

I left these pages blank for you pal.
If you have any ideas, just write them down:

www.ingramcontent.com/pod-product-compliance
Lightning Source LLC
LaVergne TN
LVHW072101070426

835508LV00002B/218

* 9 7 8 0 6 9 2 9 8 3 5 6 0 *